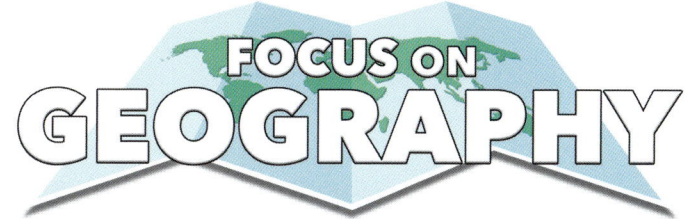

Focus on
South Africa

Natalie Hyde

www.crabtreebooks.com

Author: Natalie Hyde

Series research and development:
Janine Deschenes

Editorial director: Kathy Middleton

Editor: Janine Deschenes

Proofreader: Roseann Biederman

Design: Tammy McGarr

Print and production coordinator:
Tammy McGarr

IMAGE CREDITS
Alamy
  Peter Horree / Alamy Stock Photo: p. 4, World History Archive / Alamy Stock Photo: p. 23 (bottom right), p. 33 (top right)
Creative Commons
  p. 21 (bottom), p. 25 (top), p. 27 (bottom), Laura SA: p. 37 (top left)
Dreamstime
  Anke Van Wyk: p. 35 (bottom right)
Shutterstock
  Sunshine Seeds: front cover (top right), p. 12 (bottom), p. 29 (top), p. 34 (bottom), p. 37 (top right), p. 42 (all), p. 43 (all), p. 45 (bottom), LongJon: p. 15 (top), Mark Fisher: p. 17 (top), Angela N Perryman: p. 17 (bottom), Sopotnicki: p. 18 (bottom), Oleg Znamenskiy: p. 18 (top), Grant Duncan-Smith: p. 19 (top right), EQRoy: p. 19 (left), Jane Rix: front cover (top middle), p. 20 (top), Burhan Ay Photography: p. 21 (top), SAPhotog: p. 22, Tom Wurl: p. 23 (right middle), franco lucato: p. 24 (top right), Nico van Blerk: p. 25 (bottom middle), Snap2Art: p. 26 (bottom), Luke Schmidt: p. 26 (top), Icswart.: p. 27 (top), Grant Duncan-Smith: p. 29 (bottom), David Buzzard: p. 34 (top), InnaFelker.: p. 35 (bottom left), Gosza Wlodarczyk: p. 35 (top right), Tatyana Soares: p. 36 (top), selim kaya photography: p. 36 (bottom), Gil.K: p. 37 (bottom), Carlo Kaminski: p. 39 (top), Icswart: p. 38-39 (bottom), Alexandre G. ROSA: p. 40 (top), Gareth_Bargate: p. 44 (top)
Wikimedia Commons
  Firebrace: Plate I, The Cullinan (1908): p. 33 (top left),

All other images from Shutterstock

Library and Archives Canada Cataloguing in Publication
Available at the Library and Archives Canada

Library of Congress Cataloging-in-Publication Data
Available at the Library of Congress

Crabtree Publishing Company
www.crabtreebooks.com   1-800-387-7650
Copyright © **2023 CRABTREE PUBLISHING COMPANY**

All rights reserved. No part of this publication may be reproduced, stored in a retrieval system or be transmitted in any form or by any means, electronic, mechanical, photocopying, recording, or otherwise, without the prior written permission of Crabtree Publishing Company. In Canada: We acknowledge the financial support of the Government of Canada through the Canada Book Fund for our publishing activities.

Printed in the U.S.A./072022/CG20220201

Published in Canada
Crabtree Publishing
616 Welland Ave.
St. Catharines, Ontario
L2M 5V6

Published in the United States
Crabtree Publishing
347 Fifth Avenue
Suite 1402-145
New York, NY 10016

Contents

INTRODUCTION
Down into the Deep 4

CHAPTER 1
The Land 8

CHAPTER 2
Development 18

CHAPTER 3
Life Today 24

CHAPTER 4
A Vibrant Country 32

CHAPTER 5
Looking to the Future.......................... 40

Glossary 46

Learning More 47

Index 48

About the Author 48

INTRODUCTION

Mining contributes more to South Africa's **economy** than any other industry.

Down into the Deep

Each day, workers in the town of Musina line up to board the white buses that will take them to the Venetia Diamond Mine. The Limpopo District, where Musina is located, has over eighty diamond mines. Venetia Diamond Mine is the biggest. Some of the workers **commuting** to the mine will set the blast charges that blow up huge sections of a cliff. Some will drive massive haul trucks, each the size of a three-storey building, with tires 12 feet (3.6 m) tall. These haul trucks get filled with rock from a shovel machine that is 65 feet (19.8 m) tall and worth $30 million. Other workers will operate the machines that crush the rocks to **extract** diamonds. Still others will clean the **rough diamonds** to get them ready to be cut, polished, and made into jewelry.

Company Town

Forty percent of the workers at Venetia Diamond Mine live in Musina. Many of them live in houses built or rented by De Beers, the company that owns Venetia Mine. After work, they might eat at one of the trendy restaurants in town before watching a soccer game at the Messina Transvaal Development Stadium. Others may enjoy a motorbike rally through the beautiful surrounding area.

4

AT A GLANCE

- **OFFICIAL NAME:** Republic of South Africa
- **NATIONAL CAPITALS:** Cape Town, Pretoria, Bloemfontein
- **POPULATION:** 60,143,000
- **OFFICIAL LANGUAGES:** Afrikaans, English, Ndebele, Pedi, Sotho, Swati, Tsonga, Tswana, Venda, Xhosa, Zulu
- **LAND AREA:** 471,359 square miles (1,220,813 sq. km)

South Africa is the southernmost country on the continent of Africa. It fully surrounds the country of Lesotho, which used to be the British colony of Basutoland. Lesotho declared its independence from the United Kingdom in 1966.

Shared Duties

South Africa has three capital cities. Each has a different purpose. Pretoria is the administrative capital city. It is where the president lives and where the international embassies are found.

Cape Town is the legislative capital. It is where the government creates and upholds laws. Bloemfontein is the **judicial** capital. It is where the Supreme Court of Appeal is located.

INTRODUCTION

Parts of a Whole

South Africa is divided into nine provinces. The Northern Cape in the East is the largest province. It is mostly a **semi-arid** desert area called the Great Karoo. South of Northern Cape is Western Cape province. It contains the southernmost point on the continent of Africa called Cape Agulhas. The capital and second-largest South African city of Cape Town is also located there.

Gauteng is the smallest province but has the highest population. Many people live in Johannesburg, South Africa's largest city. Pretoria is also found there. Most of the province is a high grassland called the highveld. Limpopo is the northernmost province in South Africa. It is named after the Limpopo River, which forms its western and northern borders and has rich mineral **deposits**, such as gold, copper, and nickel.

The Great Karoo and the Little Karoo make up the Karoo, a **plateau** that covers a wide area in South Africa, also extending into the Western Cape, Eastern Cape, and Free State provinces. Sheep farming is a common practice there and is important to the area's economy.

More than 5.5 million people live in Johannesburg. The city began as a gold-mining settlement in the late 1800s.

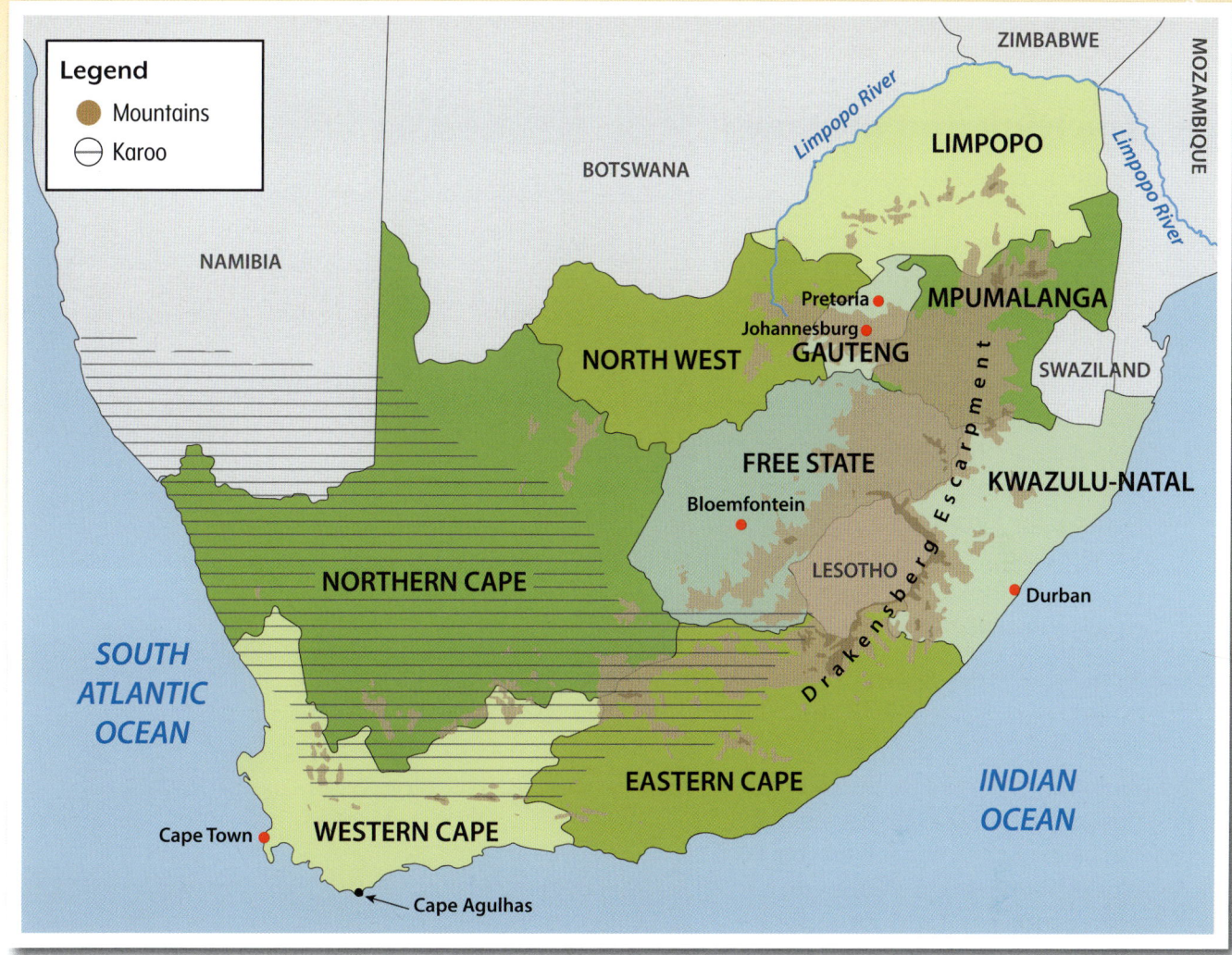

Grasslands to Mountains

North West province borders the country of Botswana. Along this border is the Magaliesberg mountain range. However, most of the province is flat, covered with scattered trees and lots of grassland. Free State province is in the interior of South Africa. Bloemfontein is located there. The land in Free State is flat and **fertile**. The province is known as South Africa's breadbasket due to its many farms. Eastern Cape province is found along South Africa's southeast coast. It is the second-largest province with several mountain ranges. The coast is mainly rocky, with a few beaches. Mpumalanga province is on the eastern border of South Africa. The Drakensberg is a steep cliff that divides this province into a high grassland in the west and a low subtropical **savannah** in the east. KwaZulu-Natal province (KZN) is about the size of Portugal and found along the southeast coast of South Africa. It is known as "the garden province." This is because it has such rich biodiversity of plants and animals. Also located in KwaZulu-Natal is the large coastal city of Durban, in which 3 million people live.

CHAPTER 1: The Land

The High and the Low

A plateau covers a large part of South Africa's interior. It has distinct areas. In the West is a semi-arid desert called the Great Karoo. The low amount of rainfall there means the soil is covered mostly with small shrubs and **succulents**. There is water under the surface that can be drilled, so the area is used for sheep farming. South of the Great Karoo is the Little Karoo, a much smaller area where the land is more fertile. Both make up the semi-desert area known as the Karoo.

To the east of the Great Karoo, the interior plateau receives slightly more rainfall. This area, called the highveld, has more fertile soil and is covered in grassland. Northeast of the highveld, the plateau has dense clusters of trees and shrubs and is called bushveld. The bushveld is one of the most mineral-rich areas in the world. Large deposits of platinum are found there.

Because of difficult living conditions, the arid areas of South Africa including the Karoo, Bushmanland, and the Kalahari Desert are sparsely populated.

Bushmanland

Great Karoo

Kalahari Desert

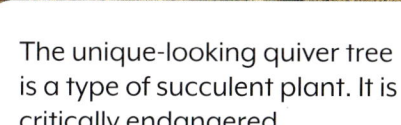

The unique-looking quiver tree is a type of succulent plant. It is critically endangered.

From Dry to Drier

The land close to the northern border is even drier than the Great Karoo. This arid land is called Bushmanland. There is very little animal and plant life there, except for the rare quiver tree. The harsh environment also means that few people live there. Because Bushmanland is so sparsely populated, Vaalputs, a nuclear waste **repository**, was located there. West of Bushmanland and north of the Great Karoo is the Kalahari Desert. The Kalahari spreads out into South Africa's northern neighbors of Botswana and Namibia. It has the nickname "thirstland" because any rain that falls quickly soaks into the sand, leaving plants and animals thirsty. Animals such as meerkats and bat-eared foxes have adapted to the lack of water and call the Kalahari home.

CHAPTER 1

The plateau was created when Earth's crust was lifted by pressure under the surface millions of years ago. The Great Escarpment is the edge of the uplifted area.

On the Edge

The boundary between the interior plateau and the narrow strip of land along the coast is the Great Escarpment. This is a steep slope that extends from the edge of the plateau down to sea level. The height of the Great Escarpment varies from about 4,921 feet (1,500 m) in the Southwest to almost 11,483 feet (3,500 m) in the East. Different sections of the Great Escarpment have different names. In the south-central province of Eastern Cape, the Great Escarpment is known as the *Sneeuberge*, or Snow Mountains. The eastern section of the Great Escarpment is known as the Drakensberg, or Dragon's Mountains.

The Garden Route

South Africa's coastline is over 1,770 miles (2,850 km) long. It extends from its northwest border with Namibia to its northeast border with Mozambique. Between the coast and the Great Escarpment is a narrow band of land called the coastal plain. In the South and Southwest, the coastal plain contains a series of mountains called the Cape Fold Mountains. These mountains were formed long before the plateau, when two **tectonic plates** pushed into each other. There is very fertile land in the long valleys between the Cape Fold Mountains. These are productive vine- and fruit-growing regions, known as the Garden Route.

Table Mountain, which rises behind Cape Town, is part of the Cape Fold Mountain range. It was named because of its flat top that resembles a table. **Indigenous** Khoisan people called it *Hoerikwaggo*, meaning "sea mountain."

Closer Look

The Cape of Good Hope was once thought to be the point where the Atlantic and Indian Oceans met. Modern geographers, however, identified this point as Cape Agulhas, the southern tip of South Africa and the African continent.

The Cape of Good Hope

At the southern tip of the Cape Peninsula, on the southwestern coast of South Africa, is the Cape of Good Hope. The first European to see the cape was Portuguese explorer Bartolomeu Dias in 1488. He first named it the Cape of Storms because of the rough seas and unpredictable weather there. It was later renamed by King John II of Portugal, who was optimistic about its place along a trade route between Europe and Asia. The Cape of Good Hope became an important port for sea travellers before a much shorter route, the Suez Canal, was established in 1869. Today, the Cape of Good Hope is a destination for tourists and a habitat for many plant and animal species.

Many shipwrecks were recorded in the rough waters around the Cape of Good Hope.

CHAPTER 1

Natural Resources

South Africa is rich in **natural resources** and is one of the world's largest sources of **raw materials**. The country is well known for its large deposits of valuable minerals. Animal and fish products are also important, due to sheep farming on the plateau and the country's access to two oceans. South Africa's unique and diverse landscape, as well as its wildlife, are other valuable natural resources. Safari and sightseeing tours, as well as water sports along the coast, boosts the economy and helps to develop settlements in these areas.

Gold, Silver, and Diamonds

South Africa is well known for its mining of diamonds and gold, but it has many other valuable minerals too. It is the world's largest producer of platinum. This mineral is used in products such as car engines, laboratory equipment, and dentistry equipment. It is also the world's largest producer of chromium and manganese, which are both used to make stainless steel.

The discovery of these mineral resources was the main reason South Africa developed such a strong economy. It also changed settlement patterns. Until the 1860s, South African towns were small. Mining, and the railways that were built to supply the mining industry, drew people into the country's interior. Cities grew as people moved to find work and better services, funded by money generated by the mining industry.

Visitors to Kruger National Park hope to see the "Big Five" of African animals: lions, leopards, rhinos, elephants, and buffalo.

Fruit and vegetables grown along the Garden Route are a valuable resource in South Africa.

Coal is another valuable mineral mined in South Africa. It provides almost all of the country's electricity.

Closer Look

The Kimberley Mine is also known as "The Big Hole." Nearly 15 million diamonds were found there. It is claimed to be the deepest human-made hole in the world.

The Kimberley Process (KP) was implemented in 2003 to make sure De Beers and other diamond companies mine and sell **conflict-free diamonds**.

Diamond Discoveries

In 1867, Erasmus Jacobs was playing near his father's farm along the Orange River near Hopetown. He found a pretty, transparent rock. It turned out to be a 21.24 carat diamond—the first diamond discovery in South Africa. A few years later, diamonds were discovered on a farm near Kimberley, in Northern Cape province. The brothers who owned the farm decided to sell the property, but their last name, de Beer, was used to name the De Beers diamond mine there. A second mine, the Kimberley, was also dug on the farm. These mines led to the Great Kimberley Diamond Rush. In the late 1800s, mines there produced more than 95 percent of the world's diamonds. Today, De Beers Group is a corporation that specializes in diamond mining and sales. South Africa was the world's sixth largest producer of diamonds in 2020.

CHAPTER 1

A Place to Settle

South Africa's population is just over 60 million people. Most of them live in the eastern and northeastern parts of the county. This is because resources such as water, fertile land, and employment are more abundant there. Southern coastal areas are also more populated. In comparison, the western region of the country is more **sparsely** populated. There is one exception: Cape Town and its surrounding area, in the southwest.

Many of the larger cities in South Africa, such as Durban and Cape Town, are near the coast. They were established because people had access to the water for food, trade, and transportation. Places farther inland in the northeast changed from towns and villages to cities as people settled there looking for work in mining and farming. A railway built in 1872 from Cape Town, then known as Cape Colony, to Kimberley allowed more people to **migrate** into the interior.

Water-pumping windmills, such as this one (above), have enabled farming and increased settlement in South Africa's semi-desert areas.

14

The Land

Some towns and cities change in population throughout the year. This is due to the migration of seasonal workers.

Informal settlements are often located outside major cities, to which people can travel to access jobs and services.

Ranch Style

The Great Karoo was mostly wild and sparsely populated until windmills were built to pump water from below the ground. These wells allowed ranchers to move in and set up vast sheep farms. Recently, **nature reserves** and game farms have been established in the Great Karoo. They have reintroduced some of the wild game that was lost because of sheep farm fencing. New projects have encouraged ranchers to remove fencing and let their animals **free range**. Removing fencing helps re-establish animals such as antelope, and the leopards and lions that hunt them. This has allowed the Great Karoo to become a tourist destination for visitors who want to see big game.

Informal Settlements

Millions of South Africans live in crowded informal settlements, in which makeshift homes are built close together on public land. Informal settlements usually lack infrastructure, such as running water, and basic services, such as health care. People in informal settlements live in poverty. Some might have been forced out of cities due to population growth and a lack of affordable housing. Others migrated there in search of jobs in urban areas or were displaced due to disasters or economic vulnerability. In South Africa, particularly, informal settlements are often a result of **apartheid** policies that **segregated** neighborhoods by race.

Cape Town earned the nickname "Mother City" because it was the first European settlement in South Africa. However, many large settlements of Indigenous Africans existed before then.

15

CHAPTER 1

The Durban beachfront is a popular spot for tourists and surfers due to its warmer, Indian Ocean waters.

Climate and Weather

Because it is surrounded by water on three sides, oceans play a major role in the climate and weather of South Africa. Oceans **regulate** land temperatures and provide moisture. One of the fastest and strongest flowing currents in the world runs just off South Africa's east coast: the Agulhas Current. This current brings warm tropical water southward, heating the land. Because the Atlantic and Indian Oceans meet at Cape Agulhas, the eastern side and western side of the country have different temperatures. Indian Ocean currents are warmer than Atlantic. That means cities such as Durban, on the east coast, are on average six degrees warmer than cities such as Port Nolloth, on the western coast—even though they are at roughly the same **latitude**.

The Cape Fold Mountains along South Africa's coast play a role in how and where there is rain. Warm air that picks up moisture from the oceans rises up the mountain. As it rises, the air cools and the moisture is released as rain or snow. This means that much of the rain falls along the narrow coastal plains, known as the Garden Route. The interior plains of South Africa are then left dry and arid.

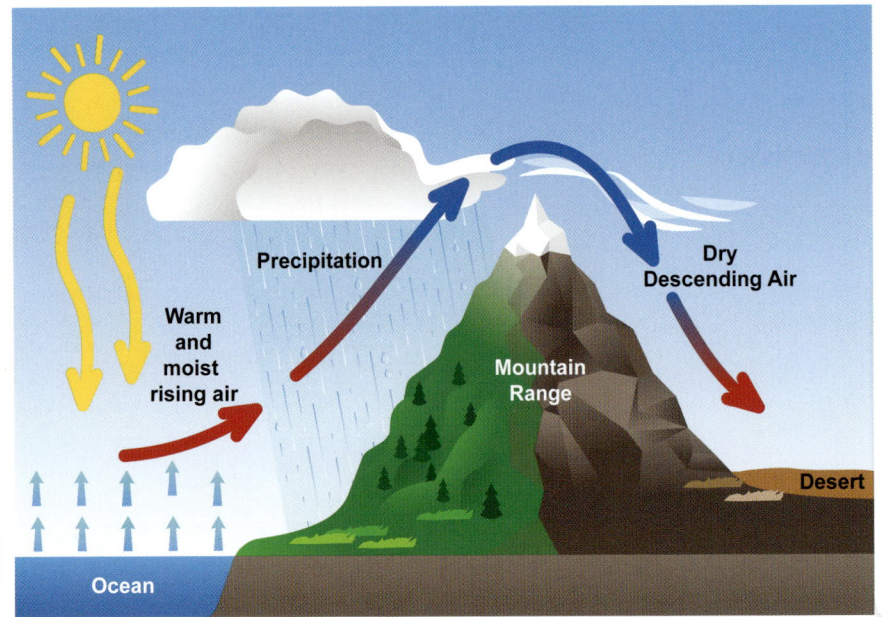

The warm ocean waters cause air to pick up moisture. As this air rises up the Great Escarpment it cools and rains, creating a lush, fertile area. As the air tops the mountains and travels down the other side, it is dry and creates arid conditions like in the Great Karoo.

16

The Land

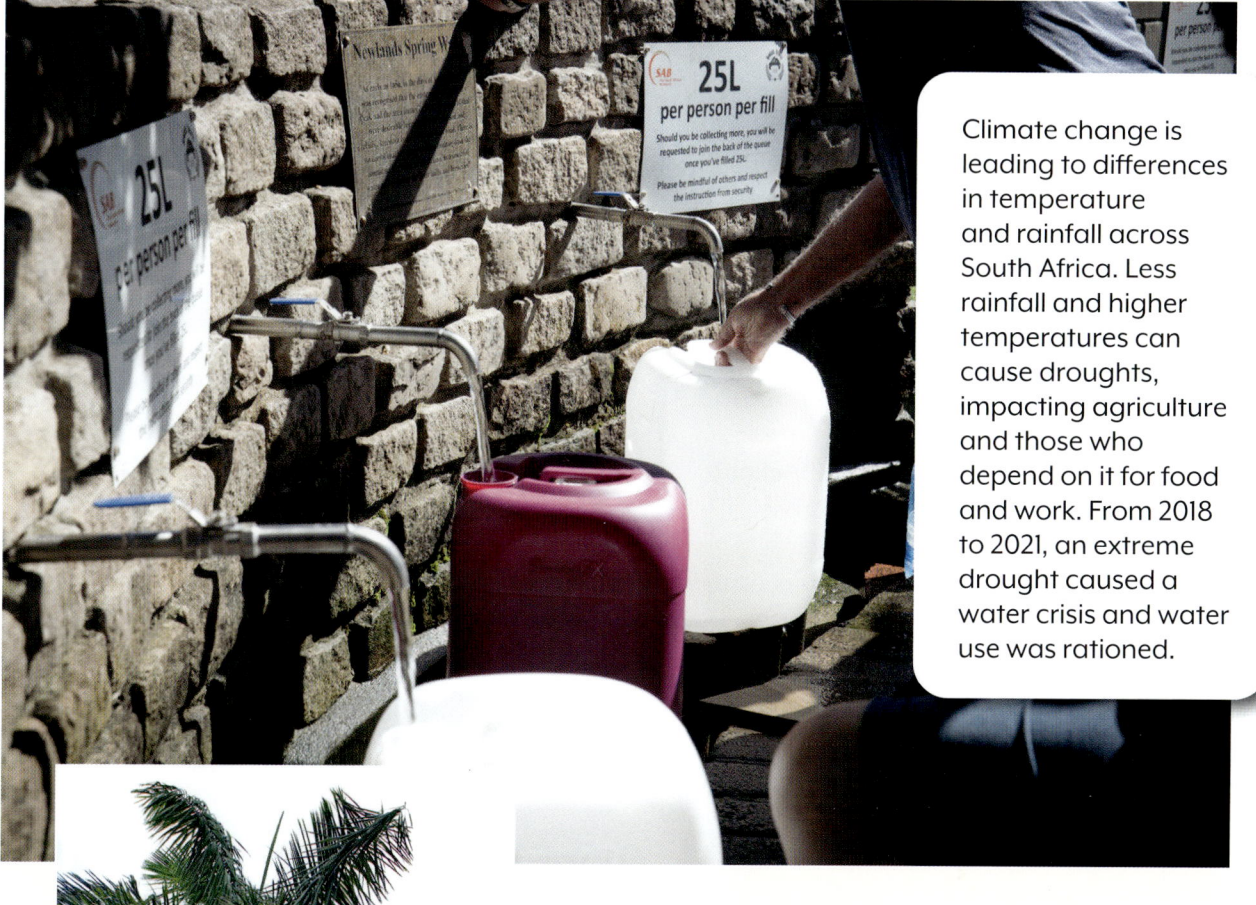

Climate change is leading to differences in temperature and rainfall across South Africa. Less rainfall and higher temperatures can cause droughts, impacting agriculture and those who depend on it for food and work. From 2018 to 2021, an extreme drought caused a water crisis and water use was rationed.

Sunny Side Up

South Africa is famous for its sunshine. It gets about 2,500 hours of it each year. Most of South Africa only gets rain in the summer. Summer in the **Southern Hemisphere** is December, January, and February. In the Cape Fold Mountains, there are freezing temperatures in the winter months. This weather allows for skiing and other winter sports. Winter is June, July, and August. The rest of the country has milder winter temperatures.

Celebrations that North Americans usually celebrate in the winter, such as Christmas, fall in South African summer. Instead of evergreen Christmas trees, palm trees are wrapped in holiday colors.

17

CHAPTER 2

Development

First Inhabitants

Africa is known as the cradle of humankind. The oldest human fossils have been found on the continent. The first inhabitants of southern Africa were Indigenous people known as the Khoisan. This is a term used to describe multiple Indigenous tribes, including the Khoekhoe and the San people, who have related languages and ethnicities. The Khoekhoe herded animals such as cattle across the plains and the San were hunter-gatherers. Over two thousand years ago, northern Bantu-speaking groups also migrated south from central Africa. They established agricultural settlements, which **displaced** many Khoisan people. Those descended from Bantu-speaking groups now make up the majority of Black Africans in South Africa.

Safe Harbor

In the 1600s, European explorers looked for a water route to trade with Asia. The Cape of Good Hope became a convenient and safe harbor to take on food and water for the long trip to Asia. In 1652, the Dutch East India Company established a settlement in what is now called Cape Town. Dutch farmers came and began to farm. They brought **enslaved** people from other parts of Africa and Asia to work as laborers. Their settlements expanded due to this forced labor. The Khoisan people, who had occupied the area for at least one thousand years prior, had refused to work for the colonizers. But as their settlements grew, they were **dispossessed** of their lands.

More than 400 ethnic Indigenous African groups speak some form of a Bantu language. In South Africa, the term "Bantu" was used to describe people during apartheid. It is offensive there today.

Khoisan people are fighting for status as the first nation in South Africa. They also want the South African government to recognize their language and traditional lands.

Closer Look

British Takeover

The British saw South Africa as an important station for trade with Asia. In 1795, they took the Cape by force. They **abolished** the colony's slave trade, or its practice of importing enslaved people, in 1807. However, enslaved people already in the colony were not freed. Slavery was banned by the British government in 1833 and finally took effect in the country's South African colony in December 1834.

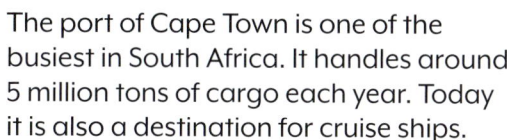

The port of Cape Town is one of the busiest in South Africa. It handles around 5 million tons of cargo each year. Today it is also a destination for cruise ships.

Dutch East India Company

When the Dutch East India Company (VOC) established a port in South Africa, many traders and merchants then settled in the area. As a permanent settlement, it also became a popular place for workers in the company to retire. The VOC encouraged the Dutch to settle near Cape Town. Its colony there was called the Cape Colony. Over time, Dutch **colonizers** and those from other European countries began to move inland to establish bigger ranches and farms. Descendants of these early settlers now identify as Afrikaners.

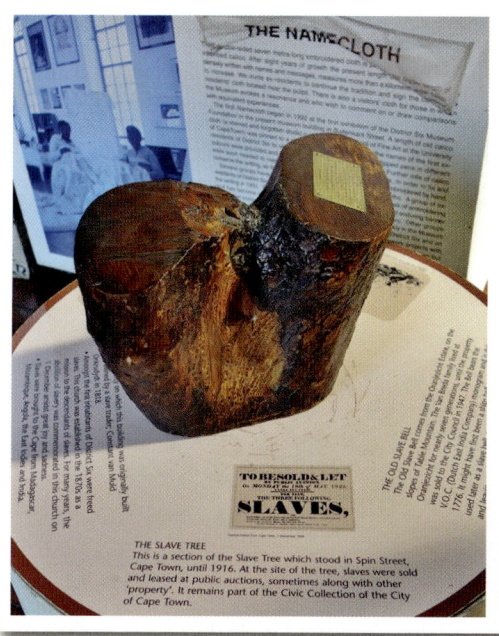

The Castle of Good Hope, built by the VOC, is the oldest colonial building in South Africa. It was built near the shoreline to help protect against possible invasions by sea.

On display at a Cape Town museum is a piece of a tree (above) under which many enslaved people were sold. Between 1652, when the Dutch East India Company established a settlement at Cape Town, and 1807, when the slave trade ended, about 60,000 enslaved people were brought to the colony.

19

CHAPTER 2

Original Settlements

Many of the cities in South Africa today grew out of Indigenous settlements. Bloemfontein, which is now the capital of Free State, was originally inhabited by the !Orana clan of Khoekhoen people. The city was officially founded when the British army chose it as a location for a fort.

As **hunter-gatherers**, the Zulu people had lived in and around what is now Durban for hundreds of thousands of years. In 1823, British traders, who had anchored there during a storm, began to trade with Shaka, king of the mighty Zulu empire. British settlers soon followed in 1824 and established a settlement there. Orginally called Port Natal by the British, it was renamed "D'Urban" after Sir Benjamin D'Urban, who was governor of Cape Colony.

Indigenous peoples historically gave Cape Town a name that meant "where clouds gather." Portuguese explorer Bartholemeu

With more than 10 million people, the Zulu are the largest ethnic group in South Africa.

Dias saw it in 1488 and re-named it Cape Town because it was near the Cape of Good Hope. The United East India Company established a way station there for their trade with Asia. The Dutch traded tobacco, copper, and iron with the Khoisan people in exchange for fresh meat and other supplies.

In the years that followed their landing at Port Natal, the British invaded Zulu territory. The Anglo-Zulu War of 1879 began after Zulu King Cetshwayo was unwilling to submit to the British. This monument, depicting a Zulu warrior's necklace, honors warriors who fought in the war's first major battle. The Zulu lost the war and did not regain their independence, despite uprisings that followed.

Development

Johannesburg is known as "The City of Gold." It is one of the 100 largest urban areas in the world.

Mineral Revolution

Other cities were founded as natural resources were discovered. When valuable minerals such as copper and diamonds were discovered in 1867, it started what historians call the Mineral Revolution. Kimberley grew out of a mining camp after diamonds were discovered there. By 1873, it was the second largest town in South Africa. Johannesburg has grown to be the largest city in South Africa thanks to the discovery of gold there in 1884. Within 10 years of the first gold find, 100,000 people flooded the area. European land and mine owners became very rich using the cheap labor of hundreds of thousands of Black Africans. Mining is still one of the biggest contributors to South Africa's economy.

Work in the mines was difficult. The temperatures were very high, the work was heavy, and miners put in 14-hour days. There were often serious accidents.

21

CHAPTER 2

Mines and Farms

The first industries in South Africa were agriculture and mining. The Dutch and the British used the areas around Cape Town and Durban as places to stop and take on supplies on their way to trade in Asia. As these trading outposts grew, European settlers came. They were **allotted** farmland, which displaced Indigenous peoples. The mining industry in South Africa began with the first copper mine in the 1850s. The discovery of diamonds in 1867 led to the Great Kimberley Diamond Rush.

The majority of these industries were owned and run by white Europeans, while Black Africans were used as cheap manual labor. The difference in wealth and opportunities became **entrenched** in society. It was one of the foundations of the separation of white and Black people in South Africa. This separation was called apartheid. Today, South Africa has a strong manufacturing sector, including textiles, electronics, and cars. While Black African ownership in companies is rising, the reality is that white Europeans still control much of the industry in South Africa.

Half a million automobiles of all types are manufactured each year in South Africa.

Closer Look

The housing areas to which non-white people were forced to move during apartheid had poor conditions. Many of these settlements remain today, as those who spent decades there had little opportunity to gain wealth and afford better housing.

Apartheid

Apartheid is the **Afrikaans** word for "separateness." It was a political and social system that began officially in 1948, although there had been a history of inequality in the country for decades. Apartheid touched every part of daily life. Eighty percent of the country's land was set aside for the white minority, in an effort to protect this group's wealth, jobs, and culture.

Non-white people, including Black Africans, Asians, and those with mixed race, were forced to live in "Black homelands." Many were forcibly removed from homes in areas designated for white people. Hospitals, ambulances, buses, and public facilities were all segregated by race. The racist system lasted for decades. There were protests, strikes, demonstrations, and eventually, armed resistance. Finally, with increased international pressure, changes began and the laws that allowed segregation were **repealed** between 1990 and 1994. In 1994, Nelson Mandela, who had been imprisoned for 27 years for protesting apartheid, was elected the first Black president. It was the first time every South African citizen had the right to vote.

The entrance to the Apartheid Museum in Johannesburg reminds visitors of the segregation that touched every part of life.

One method of resistance was striking, since the white minority largely relied on the labor of non-white workers.

CHAPTER 3
Life Today

Although apartheid was formally ended in 1994, it still affects the life of South Africans today. South Africa is called the "most unequal nation on the planet." How and where people live is still largely dependent on their race and **ethnicity**. Bigger South African cities have all of the same modern conveniences and entertainment as other countries. However, not everyone can enjoy them. Most white people live in wealthy neighborhoods while Black and other non-white people usually live in poorer townships with a lack of decent sewage, water, or reliable power.

South Africa is considered a developing country. Developing countries have a lower average income than developed countries such as Canada or the United States. Developing countries also have limited access to quality health care and education. South Africa is at this level because although it has abundant goods and natural resources, there are still high unemployment and poverty rates. This may change in the future as South Africa improves hospitals, education, power plants, and trade relations.

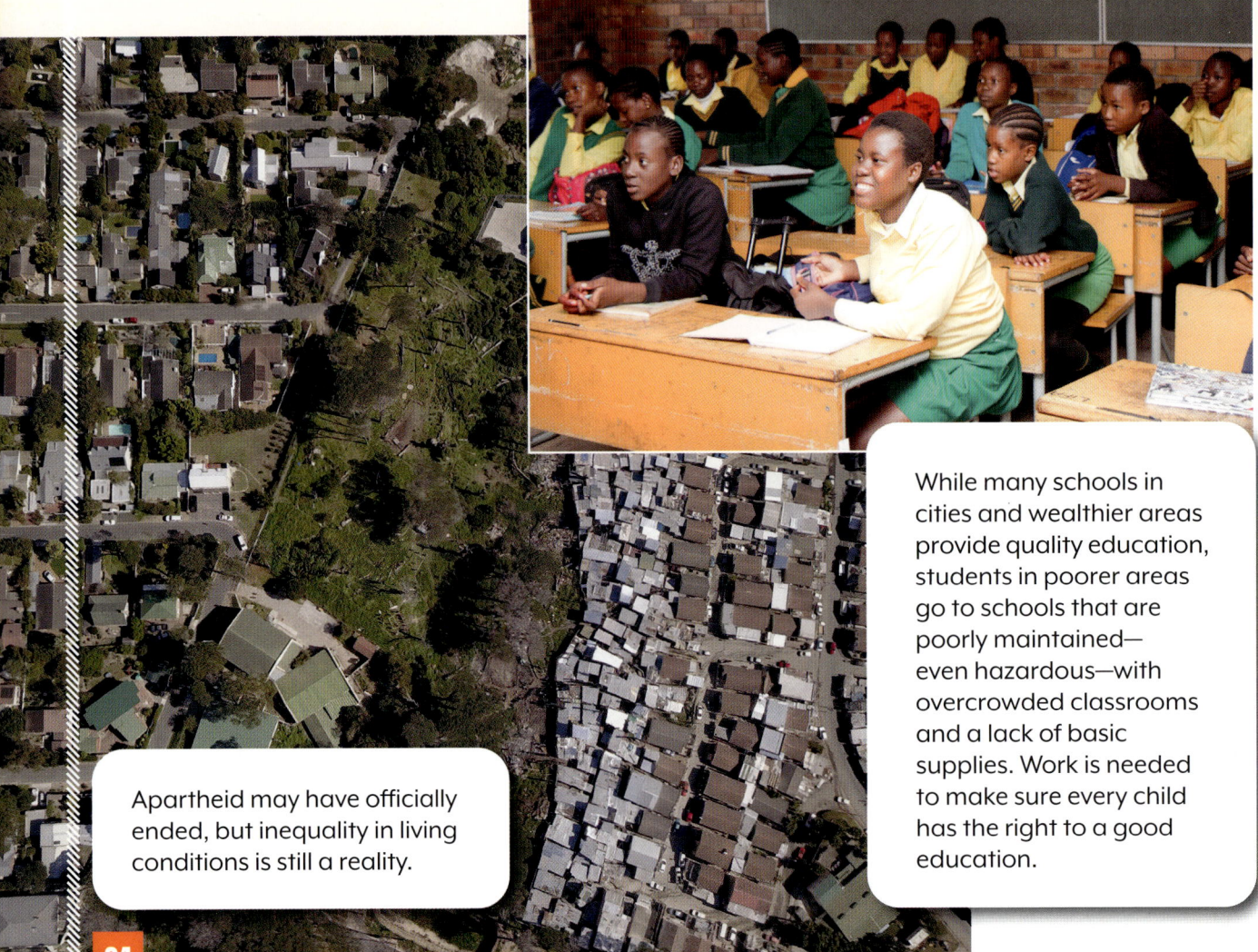

Apartheid may have officially ended, but inequality in living conditions is still a reality.

While many schools in cities and wealthier areas provide quality education, students in poorer areas go to schools that are poorly maintained—even hazardous—with overcrowded classrooms and a lack of basic supplies. Work is needed to make sure every child has the right to a good education.

Closer Look

Nelson Mandela

Nelson Mandela became involved in politics in South Africa in 1942 to fight for equality for Black Africans. He helped to form the African National Congress Youth League. His political protests and actions led to his arrest and sentence of life imprisonment in 1964. He served 27 years in the prison on Robben Island. When he was finally released in 1990, he went back to work to end white minority rule through talks with the president of South Africa. In 1993 he and President F.W. de Klerk jointly won the Nobel Peace Prize for their work in ending apartheid. In April 1994, he voted for the first time in his life. The following May, he was **inaugurated** as South Africa's first democratically elected and first non-white president. He stepped down in 1999 after one term, but continued his advocacy for social justice through the Nelson Mandela Foundation, which he established that year. He died in his home in Johannesburg in 2013.

As president, Nelson Mandela and his government focused on dismantling apartheid and working to end racism. It also encouraged post-apartheid **reconciliation**, in part by establishing the Truth and Reconciliation Commission (TRC) in 1995. Made up of many members of the public, it gathered evidence about injustices, recorded victim statements, and recommended measures to avoid future human rights violations.

Mandela Day is an international holiday observed on July 18, Mandela's birthday, each year. It encourages people around the world to act against injustices and **inequities** in their communities.

25

CHAPTER 3

Watching professional sports is one way that South African people come together.

Sports and Recreation

South Africans are big sports fans. The flat interior plain of South Africa means there are lots of places for field sports such as cricket, football—or soccer—rugby, and golf. South Africa is one of the few countries that has hosted the World Cup competitions for three major sports: cricket, football, and rugby. To play for the Proteas (cricket), Springboks (rugby), or Bafana Bafana (football) national teams is a source of great pride in South Africa.

Skiing in Africa?

Most people don't think of a trip to South Africa for skiing. However, the Drakensburg Mountains section of the Great Escarpment is high enough and cold enough from June to August for some fun winter sports. In the summer months of December to February, ski resorts are still open so visitors can enjoy mountain biking, fly fishing, hiking, and rock climbing. South Africa also has some regional and traditional sports. Ringball is a South African version of netball. In both games, players pass a ball between each other and try to get it in a net, similar to basketball.

Cricket is a popular sport around the world, especially in countries such as India, Australia, New Zealand, and South Africa. It is similar to baseball.

Ringball has been played for more than 100 years in South Africa. Over time, the rules were adapted to be more suitable for girls and women. This new version of ringball is called korfball.

26

Life Today

Thousands of runners enter the race each year. In 2019, 25,000 athletes competed.

Biggest, Baddest Road Race

The remote distances between cities across the plains have also made South Africa the perfect place for the Comrades Marathon, also called The Ultimate Human Race. This is an **ultramarathon** of about 56 miles (89 km). It is run between Durban, on the east coast, and Pietermaritzburg, the capital city of KwaZulu-Natal province. It started in 1921, making it the world's oldest and largest ultramarathon race. Each year the direction of the race changes, challenging runners to run either "up" from sea level in Durban to the interior plain, or "down" from Pietermaritzburg to the coast. The route also has a series of five hills, the highest being 2,850 ft (870 km). The top ten fastest men and the top ten fastest women get gold medals and bragging rights.

27

CHAPTER 3

Digging Down

Mining is still the biggest industry in South Africa today, employing around half a million people. Statistics show that for every person in the country's mining industry, there is an average of nine other people who depend on them financially.

Diamond resources are mostly found in the East and Northeast. These deposits are far from **depleted**. The country's three largest mines, Venetia, Finsch, and Kimberley, have new developments that will expand production and keep the mines open and running for another 25 to 50 years. Also in the northeast of the country is a **formation** called the Witwatersrand Basin. It is a rocky plateau that rises above the interior plain. The Basin is a major source of gold. Some gold mines in this area have reached depths of 4,000 meters (13, 123 ft). The Deep South gold mine is one of the largest and deepest in the world.

South Africa is one of the world's top producers of gold.

Diamond mining in South Africa has been operating for more than 150 years. The country's diamond exports were valued at more than 1.5 billion in 2016.

Life Today

Platinum and the Bushveld Complex

Platinum is a silvery-white metal that is often used for jewelry, but its main use is in catalytic converters in cars, trucks, and buses. These devices turn the toxic gases from engines into less harmful **emissions**. The world's largest open pit platinum mine is found in Limpopo province. It was dug into the Bushveld Complex, which is a layer of **igneous rock**. The Bushveld Complex also has other valuable elements such as chromium and vanadium.

The Dirty Side of Mining

The mining industry does not come without problems. It contributes to air and water pollution, such as **acid mine drainage**. Toxic waste and abandoned mines pose risks to South African communities. Environmental destruction is the biggest impact of mining. Reversing this destruction is slow and difficult because the laws are unclear about who is responsible for the cost and the time to clean up and restore the land. People who live in mining communities often deal with harmful air pollution. Others are forced to relocate when land is allocated for mining. This often means they lose important farmland or grazing lands for their animals.

Platinum is generally more difficult to mine than gold because it is located deeper in the earth.

Mining activities can endanger South African wildlife by destroying or polluting habitats. Researchers are concerned about threats to biodiversity in the country.

CHAPTER 3

Nguni cattle have long been the cornerstone of traditional Zulu culture. They were given symbolic importance and were often exchanged as gifts.

Farming the Land

Even though much of the land in South Africa is arid and infertile, agricultural activities are very important to the country's economy. Indigenous peoples in South Africa have traditionally raised cattle for meat and milk, and still do today. Nguni are a breed of cattle unique to South Africa. The breed was brought there by groups of Bantu-speaking people from the North of Africa. There are about 14 million **head** of cattle in South Africa today. When the British and Dutch began to settle the interior plain, they brought sheep with them. Today there are about 8,000 sheep farms in the Great Karoo and 28 million sheep. They are raised for wool and meat.

The Dorper, an Indigenous South African sheep breed, has been bred to survive the hot and arid Karoo region. It now is valued worldwide for its **hardiness**.

Life Today

National parks in the Karoo, such as the Tankwa Karoo National Park, help maintain the region's biodiversity and encourage wildlife restoration. One initiative there involves reintroducing varieties of antelope to the area.

Keeping the Karoo Green

Large numbers of sheep herds can cause problems in the interior plains. Sheep and goats eat the grass down, leaving nothing but bare dirt. These areas can then be easily blown away by wind, causing **soil erosion**. Long ago, the Karoo was covered in grass and was much greener. This was due in part to migrating antelopes. Their hooves broke up the soil's surface and their droppings fertilized it. New projects in the Karoo are encouraging farmers to imitate the antelope migration by keeping the sheep moving. Doing so makes sure that the sheep eat only the tops of the grass and means that their droppings fertilize a wider area of soil.

Another problem in the Karoo is that livestock fences stop wildlife from roaming free. Today "no fence grazing" is being studied to see if it helps promote plant biodiversity and allows wildlife to return. So far, this method shows thicker plant growth and the slow return of wild animals.

Ostriches are well suited to dry, arid conditions such as those in the Great Karoo. Ostrich farms in South Africa provide feathers as well as leather and meat to markets around the world.

CHAPTER 4
A Vibrant Country

South Africa has an important place in the continent of Africa. It generates two thirds of Africa's electricity. Most of that is with coal-fired power plants. However, a plan is in place to reduce the use of coal for power by 36 percent by the year 2040 and replace it with wind and solar power generation.

Protecting Wildlife Diversity

South Africa plays a large role in the conservation and protection of wildlife. It is home to more kinds of mammals than North and South America combined. Kruger National Park is the largest in South Africa and has a wide variety of wildlife species, from big cats to rare birds and the endangered black rhino. This park is about the size of the state of Massachusetts. In 1991, South Africa also became the first country in the world to protect the Great White Shark.

The yellow-breasted pipit is **endemic** to South Africa and is found in the grasslands of the Drakensberg mountains. Commercial livestock farming is causing habitat loss, however. Nature reserves in the area aim to protect the species and its habitat.

Chances are, if you buy fruit at your local grocery store, some of it is imported from South Africa. South Africa is the second-largest exporter of fruit in the world. Oranges, grapes, apples, and lemons are some of the most highly exported fruits. Not all grapes grown in South Africa are exported, however. They are turned into wine. South Africa has the oldest wine industry outside of Europe.

South Africa is the world's second-largest exporter of citrus fruits. These fruits are grown across the country.

32

Sparkling Reputation

South Africa is known for its diamonds because the De Beers Group controls more than 80 percent of the world supply of rough diamonds. South Africa is also the biggest producer of platinum in the world. The Zondereinde platinum mine in Limpopo province is the deepest in the world. Out of the Jagersfontein mine, in Free State, came two of the ten largest diamonds ever discovered. One is the Excelsior diamond, which is 972 carats. The other is the Queen Victoria's Jubilee diamond, at 245 carats.

Jubilee diamond

Rough Cullinan diamond

The Cullinan Diamond mine (below) near Pretoria, South Africa, has produced the largest diamond ever found: the Cullinan Diamond, at 3,106 carats!

CHAPTER 4

A Diverse National Culture

The culture of South Africa is one of the most diverse in the world. There are 11 official languages representing the many different Indigenous groups of the area as well as the Europeans and Asians that settled there. The major ethnic groups in South Africa today include Zulu, Basotho, Venda, Xhosa, Tsonga, Khoikhoi, Ndebele, and San. Bantu-speaking people form the major part of the population—about 35 million.

The specialty food found in South Africa also reflects the country's blend of cultures. *Chakalaka* is a vegetable relish that is traditionally served with pap, a kind of porridge made from maize. *Bobotie* is a national dish of baked meat with an egg topping that originated in East Asia. *Melktert*, a custard-filled pastry, is an Afrikaner dish of Dutch origin. *Biltong* and *droëwors* are traditional Indigenous smoked, dried meats.

In modern cities, many traditions are being slowly lost. However, a new culture is forming. It combines Western and traditional cultures and is evident in art, music, and food.

Shisa nyama, which is Zulu for "burn the meat," is a term used for places or events where barbequed meat, known as *braais*, is served. Shisa nyamas are vibrant places that bring communities together to enjoy food, music, and fun.

34

Closer Look

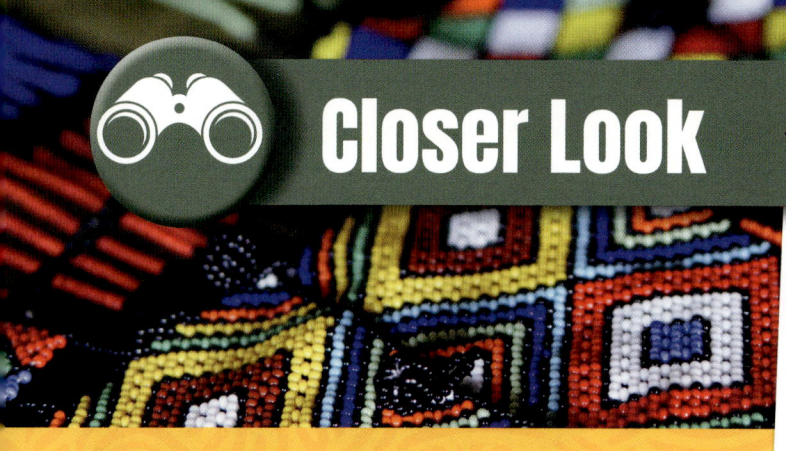

A Rainbow Nation

The different strengths and skills of South Africa's diverse ethnic groups create one of the most unique national cultures in the world. Indigenous cultures there are wide and varied, and can be seen through diverse traditions and customs.

The Khoekhoen and San are known for their tracking skills. They use these skills today against poachers of endangered animals, such as rhinoceros.

Zulus are shield bearing warriors. They are also famous for beadwork and basketry.

The Xhosa have a strong **oral tradition** and are storytellers of tales about **ancestral** heroes.

Beads have special significance in Zulu culture. Different bead patterns and colors have specific meanings, such as a person's marital status or feelings of anger, love, jealousy, and contentment.

The Ndebele decorate their homes in beautiful **geometric** designs.

Sotho people have a unique way of organizing their villages. People are grouped into "age sets" with different responsibilities so all the needs of the community are met.

The Venda are a spiritual people. They believe lakes and rivers are sacred and rains are controlled by a Python God.

These Sotho women wear mokorotlo, traditional cone-shaped straw hats.

The geometric designs on Ndebele houses were actually a form of communication or an expression of emotion or resistance.

CHAPTER 4

Art in South Africa

In the countryside, music is a vital part of cultural life. Many songs in the country speak of the struggles and **discrimination** of apartheid.

Traditionally, Indigenous groups, including the Nguni, Sotho, and Venda, performed *ingoma* or "dance-songs" as well as drumming. Rhythmic work songs helped with trench-digging or cattle-herding. Some were seasonal rituals, such as harvesting songs. Music also played a central role in rites and ceremonies such as weddings and burials. Song was later used as a form of resistance against cultural oppression by European enslavers and, later, a government dominated by Afrikaners. During apartheid, music was a way to unite Black citizens and promote liberation.

Today, South African music has developed into a fusion of cultures. Popular styles, such as jazz, combine with traditional music such as *isicathamiya*, a type of choral singing originating in Zulu communities.

Music is an important part of urban culture in South Africa.

There are more than 70 genres of Indigenous dance-song, ranging from large, collective events to individual performances.

A Vibrant Country

Boots on the Ground

South Africa is known for its gumboot dance. Unlike traditional dances that are thousands of years old, this type of dance got its start in the gold mines in the mid-1800s. Enslaved workers were not allowed to talk while down in the mines. The mines were often damp and partially flooded, so the workers wore rubber boots, called gumboots. They created their own secret code of stamps, slaps, and rattling of ankle chains to communicate with one another. This developed into a working class South African art form.

The gumboot dance is both a form of art and a form of resistance against oppression.

Fashion Scene

South African fashion is exploding onto the world scene. Just like South African food is a fusion of cultures, new designers are creating their own unique styles by combining traditional prints, patterns, and colors with modern tastes. Traditional beadwork was once used for ceremonial outfits or even as messages such as love letters among the Swazi and Zulu. Today, the South African craft work industry employs around one million people. The crafts are exported around the world.

South African fashion designers, such as Thabo Khumalo (above), are bringing their style to the world.

Visual art, such as paintings, murals, and drawings, is also undergoing a change as South African society shifts from apartheid to more equality across different ethnic backgrounds.

37

CHAPTER 4

Rock art in the Drakensberg mountains, made by the San, depict scenes of life as hunter-gatherers. They are an important part of South Africa's history and are treasures of the country's art.

The First Wave

The first changes to South African culture occurred with the Bantu migrations about 2,000 years ago. Bantu-speaking people left west Africa and spread out across the continent, including into South Africa. They brought new skills with them to the hunter-gatherer society that lived there. These new skills included sophisticated farming, pottery making, and iron **smelting** to make tools and weapons with metal. The need for charcoal for smelting meant forests began to be cut down. Villages became larger and more organized into kingships. Some Khoisan people were driven from their lands and retreated to even more remote areas.

A Vibrant Country

A Question of Identity

Europeans who colonized South Africa in the 1800s brought more changes. The Zulu were farmers and ranchers. Their identity was based on their lands and their family. When Europeans settled and opened mines, that identity and belief in their kings, chiefs, and warrior system was largely lost as they became laborers for European mine owners.

European settlers, merchants, soldiers, and farmers enslaved many Indigenous people, uprooting them from their native regions in South Africa and introducing other enslaved people from Madagascar, Indonesia, and India. This has contributed to the spread and fusion of traditions and cultures seen in food, clothing, music, and art.

Apartheid further divided the country and changed the culture, deepening the divide between classes and races. Some ethnic traditions and practices were driven underground, or lost all together, as Indigenous groups were forbidden to express them or had to focus their time and energy on finding ways to keep themselves and their families safe. A national identity for South Africans has been a struggle and full of conflict due to this history. The government is trying to encourage a unified national identity through **integration** and a common national future.

Finding common ground, such as by celebrating World Cup Soccer, is one way South Africans embrace a shared identity.

South Africa's holidays commemorate its history and wide population. Freedom Day is celebrated on April 27. It celebrates the first post-apartheid election, in which all South Africans were free to vote. On Heritage Day, September 24, South Africans celebrate their diverse culture. Events that promote cultural traditions, knowledge, skills, and more are held throughout the country.

CHAPTER 5
Looking to the Future

The future of South Africa could be one of amazing growth and opportunities. How South Africa positions itself in the world will depend on how it tackles some of the complex problems it is facing such as inequality, poverty, and climate change. Addressing these issues will help foster a new national identity.

One of the changes that will impact the future of South Africa is land use. Today, the majority of white South Africans still live in cities in wealthy suburbs and own the majority of businesses and industries. Black Africans mostly live in segregated townships and in poor rural areas. The country needs new laws about land use and boundaries to move to a more **inclusive** type of city planning. It also needs to prioritize equal opportunities. However, in many urban areas, landowners are using old planning laws to restrict and control new developments.

To combat the post-apartheid urban segregation, the city of Johannesburg focused on creating "corridors of freedom." In these areas, the city added better public transportation options, such as direct bus transit, and infrastructure, such as new bridges and bicycle lanes, to make it easier for people to travel between neighborhoods, especially for work. It also partnered with developers to create affordable housing along these corridors.

Ensuring that all people have equal access to well-paying jobs is one way to address deep-rooted inequities in South Africa.

40

Natural Beauty

Protecting South Africa's natural beauty and plant and animal diversity needs to be a priority in the coming years. A new conservation area is being created to help achieve this goal. Namaqualand is an arid region along the west coast of South Africa. Its new conservation area will protect 54 plant species and 64 insect species on the critically endangered list. These species cannot be found anywhere else on Earth.

Conservation South Africa is an organization that is working towards a future where humans live in harmony with nature. This will be accomplished by promoting sustainable land use, in which agricultural land can also allow for healthy ecosystems. They also promote **resilience** to climate change by encouraging landowners to set aside conservation land and commit to greener economic development.

Conservation South Africa believes that healthy ecosystems lead to healthy food. By promoting conservation in farming, they also aim to tackle food insecurity.

Namaqualand is known for its beautiful wild flowers and is a popular tourist region.

41

CHAPTER 5

Industrial Future

As with any country, South Africa's industries will shift and change as world events, politics, and environmental factors change. The natural resources that fuel the mining industry may be used up or the demand for them may alter. A stable society will contribute to an increase in manufacturing as corporations are more likely to choose to operate in the country. However, political unrest or social conflict will make the country less desirable to foreign investors.

Agricultural Challenges

Climate change and the protection of nature's diversity will mean changes in agriculture, too. Farming and agriculture practices will focus on finding and retaining water. Livestock will be bred to be able to survive on drier, less fertile grasslands. Keeping grasses growing to limit soil erosion when rainfall decreases is another way farmers and ranchers are trying to prepare for a very different future. Finding new markets for fruits and vegetables, not only in Europe, but also in other countries in Africa is key.

Teaching children about eco-friendly farming practices, such as growing local foods, is one way to promote sustainable agriculture.

A large part of South African manufacturing is making food and beverage products.

42

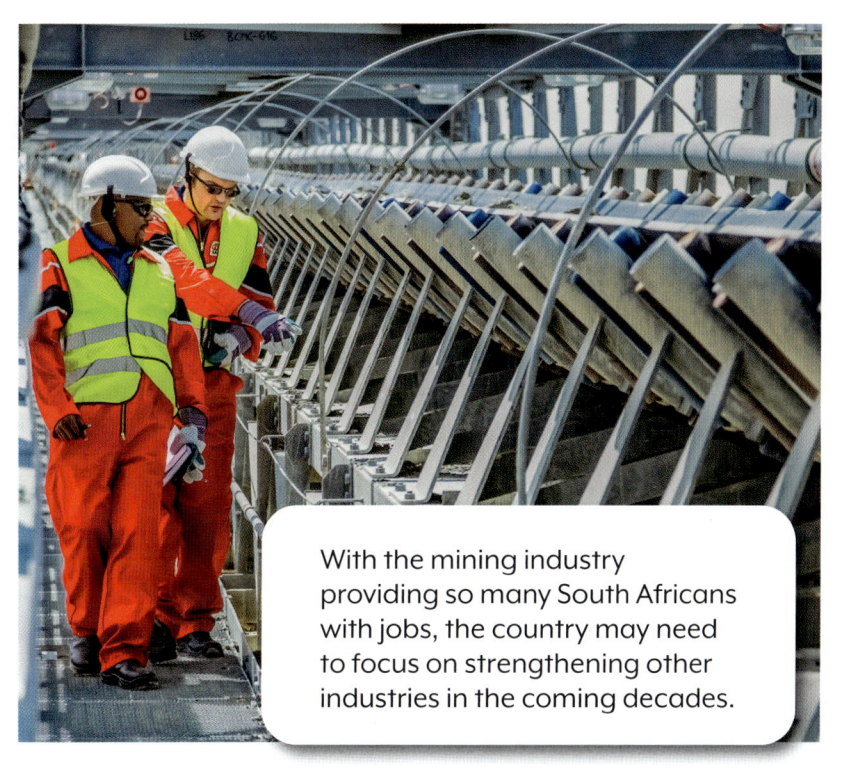

Looking to the Future

Dwindling Supply

Mineral resources don't last forever. Many of the largest mines in South Africa are being rapidly depleted. Even though South Africa has some of the largest deposits in the world, gold may run out in only 40 years, coal is expected to run out in 120 years, and platinum in less than 240. While that may seem like a long time, just the idea of a resource running out has **consequences** in the economy. Rumors of depleting supply can drive prices up, cut foreign investments, and cause unemployment.

With the mining industry providing so many South Africans with jobs, the country may need to focus on strengthening other industries in the coming decades.

Shift in Ownership

South Africa's industries are also experiencing a shift in ownership. While white Africans only make up about 9 percent of the population, they own around 90 percent of the largest companies and about 67 percent of the top positions in those businesses. President Cyril Ramaphosa and mineral resources minister, Gwede Mantashe, are proposing a plan to ensure 30 percent of companies are owned by Black South Africans by 2023.

Black African entrepreneurs such as Sibusiso Ngwenya (right), founder of Skinny Sbu Socks, and Hlangulani Msomi (left), founder of Indayi Communications, are slowly changing the balance of South African business owners.

43

CHAPTER 5

Future Changes and Challenges

One of the biggest challenges for South Africa is closing the gap between rich and poor and between races. These inequalities can still lead to violence such as riots in the KwaZulu-Natal and Gauteng provinces in July 2021. The arrest of former President Jacob Zuma due to **contempt of court** triggered protests. The protests escalated to violence as people rose up in response to inequality and poverty that persisted after apartheid. People were also grappling with high unemployment made worse by the COVID-19 pandemic.

The July 2021 riots led to widespread destruction, such as this burned warehouse in Durban. More than 100 shopping malls were looted and destroyed, and more than 300 people were killed. The riots are one indication that measures to address the widespread inequality in South Africa are needed.

Angry Climate

Throughout most of South Africa, the climate is already a challenge with large arid and semi-arid areas. Villages and farms deal with droughts and flash floods regularly. Even small changes in average temperatures can make these conditions much worse. Scientists believe that the average temperature in South Africa will rise by two to three degrees by 2050. This may have a terrible impact on industries such as agriculture, where crops will fail. Tourism will also be affected where there is a loss of biodiversity for tours or safaris. Changing weather patterns can also result in the closure of sports facilities that rely on certain weather conditions, such as skiing in the Drakensberg Mountains.

Higher temperatures and less rainfall in South Africa can lead to droughts and **desertification**, destroying fertile land and threatening the country's important agriculture industry. Desertification can also reduce biodiversity in the country, which harms its tourist industry.

44

Looking to the Future

Power Struggle

South Africa has been participating in climate change negotiations. However, it is also a major contributor. The use of coal-fired plants to make power means South Africa is the largest emitter of carbon dioxide (CO2) in the whole continent of Africa. As the country looks to reduce the gap between wealth and poverty, it will need to grow and improve infrastructure such as roads, communication, water networks, and sanitation. In order to do this, its use of power will increase and therefore its emissions. Balancing the **urgency** to bring about social equity, politics, and opportunities while lowering **carbon emissions** is the major challenge that will shape the future of South Africa.

Initiatives in South Africa are aiming to keep ecosystems healthy by removing invasive plants and replanting trees. Restoring ecosystems in this way helps tackle soil **erosion** and land **degradation** so that it can continue to be used for agriculture.

Around 77 percent of South Africa's energy comes from coal. South Africa produces 92 percent of all the coal used in the continent of Africa.

GLOSSARY

abolished Formally ended

acid mine drainage The flow of harmful acidic water from mining sites

Afrikaans A language that evolved from Dutch and is spoken mostly in southern Africa

allotted Given out shares to someone

ancestral Relating to origin or background

apartheid The government system in South Africa that segregated people by race

carbon emissions Releases of carbon into the atmosphere. Carbon is a chemical element. Carbon compounds such as carbon dioxide contribute to climate change.

colonizers Countries that take control of other countries or areas by occupying them

commuting Travelling some distance to work

conflict-free diamonds Diamonds that are mined and shipped without any connection to wars, violence, and rebel or terror groups

consequences Results of actions

contempt of court The offense of defying, or not following, a court's orders

degradation Deteriorating or making something worse or weaker

depleted Supply is used up

deposit A natural accumulation of minerals in the earth

desertification The process by which fertile land becomes desert, often due to drought and improper land use

discrimination Unjust treatment of people based on their race, age, gender, or other identifier

displaced Forced to leave one's home

dispossessed Deprived of land or possessions

economy The production and consumption of goods in a country

emissions Gases or radiation given off into the atmosphere

endemic Found only in a certain place

enslaved People without rights or choice who are forced to work without pay

entrenched Firmly established and hard to change

erosion Gradually wearing away

ethnicity Belonging to a group with a common cultural background

extract To remove or take out

fertile Able to produce crops

formation A body of rock with certain characteristics

free range Of animals, move about freely

geometric Decorated with regular lines and shapes

hardiness Able to withstand difficult conditions

head One animal in a herd

hunter-gatherers People who move from place to place to find food

igneous rock Rocks formed when magma cools

inaugurated Began a term in public office

inclusive Not leaving out any groups

Indigenous Native to a particular place. Indigenous people are the original inhabitants of a place.

inequities Injustices or unfairness

integration Blending together

judicial Relating to the court or justice system

latitude The distance north or south from the equator

migrate Move from one place to another

natural resources Materials or living things in or on the ground that can be used or sold

nature reserves Areas closed to development to protect plants and animals living there

46

LEARNING MORE

oral tradition Passing on knowledge, art, ideas, and culture through words and stories

plateau A flat area that is higher in altitude than the surrounding land

raw materials Basic, unprocessed materials from which products are made

reconciliation Efforts made to address and rectify harm done so that people or groups can resolve a conflict

regulate Control or adjust to fit certain rules or standards

repealed Removed or reversed

repository A place where things are stored

resilience Ability to recover quickly from difficulties

rough diamonds Diamond rocks that have not been cut

savannah Grassy plains

segregated Separated or divided

semi-arid A dry area, but with a little more rain than a desert

smelting Melting rock to reveal metals inside

Southern Hemisphere The part of Earth that is south of the equator

sparsely Thinly scattered

soil erosion The gradual wearing away of top layers of soil

succulents Plants able to live in dry areas by storing water in their tissues

tectonic plates Huge masses of rocks that form Earth's crust

ultramarathon A running race that is longer than a regular marathon

urgency Needing quick action

Books

Dakers, Diane. *Nelson Mandela: South Africa's Anti-Apartheid Revolutionary.* Crabtree Publishing, 2014.

Mace, Virginia. *National Geographic Countries of the World: South Africa.* National Geographic Kids, 2008.

Perritano, John. *South Africa: Tradition, Culture, and Daily Life.* Mason Crest Publishers, 2015.

Websites

https://www.natgeokids.com/uk/discover/geography/countries/facts-about-south-africa/

Check out this National Geographic site for more facts about South Africa.

https://www.nelsonmandela.org/content/page/biography

Learn about the amazing life of anti-apartheid revolutionary Nelson Mandela.

https://www.apartheidmuseum.org/permanent-exhibition

Explore the online apartheid exhibition at Johannesburg's Apartheid Museum.

INDEX

Afrikaners 19, 36
agriculture 12, 32, 42
Agulhas Current 16
Anglo-Zulu War 20
apartheid 15, 24–25, 39
artwork 35, 37, 38

Bantu-speaking peoples 18, 30, 38
biodiversity 7, 29, 31, 44
Black Africans 18, 22–23, 25, 39, 40, 43
British colonizers 19–20
bushveld 8, 29

Cape of Good Hope 11
Cape Town 6, 14–15
climate 8–9, 16–17
climate change 17, 42, 44–45
coastline 10, 16
colonization 18–19
Comrades Marathon 27
conservation 32, 41
culture 34–39

dance 37
De Beers Group 13, 33
de Klerk, F.W. 25
desert 8
desertification 44
diamonds 4, 12–13, 28, 33
Dutch colonizers 19
Dutch East India Company 18–19

economy 4, 6, 12, 21
ecosystems 41, 45
education 24
employment 4, 14–15, 22, 40, 43
energy sources 12, 32, 45
European explorers 18–19, 39
exports 12, 32–33

farming 6, 30–31
fashion 37
foods 34

geography 7–10
gold 6, 21, 28, 43
government 18, 25
Great Escarpment 10
Great Karoo 6, 8, 15

highveld 8
holidays 17, 39
hunter-gatherers 18, 20, 38

identity 39
Indigenous peoples 18, 35–36
industries 22, 28–29, 42–43

Jacobs, Erasmus 13
Johannesburg 6, 21, 23, 40

Kalahari Desert 9
Khoisan peoples 10, 18, 20
Khumalo, Thabo 37
Kimberley Mine 13, 28
Kimberley Process (KP) 13

languages 5, 18
Limpopo River 6, 7
Little Karoo 6, 8

Mandela, Nelson 25
Mantashe, Gwede 43
map of South Africa 5, 7
migration 14–15, 18, 38
mineral deposits 6, 12, 28–29

mining 4, 12–13, 21–22, 28–29
mountain ranges 10, 16
music 36

national capitals 5
natural resources 12, 43
nature reserves 15, 41
Nobel Peace Prize 25

plants 8–9, 41
plateaus 6, 8
platinum 29, 33
pollution 29, 45
population 5, 14
poverty 15, 24, 45
provinces 6

Ramaphosa, Cyril 37

seasons 17
segregation 15, 40
settlements 15, 18, 20, 23
slavery 18–19
sports 17, 26–27

transportation 40
tribes 18
Truth and Reconciliation Commission (TRC) 25

Venetia Diamond Mine 4, 28

wildlife 9, 12, 31, 32

Zulu peoples 20, 34–35

About the Author

Natalie Hyde has written over 100 fiction and non-fiction books for young readers. Exploring new cultures, traditions, and of course, food, is something she loves to do on her travels.